FROM STRUGGLE TO SUCCESS

TRANSFORMING URBAN SCHOOLS WITH
STUDENT VOICE AND EQUITY

THE SNEAKER PRINCIPAL EDUCATIONAL
LEADERSHIP SERIES

UCHE L. NJOKU, EDM

To the students whose curiosity and creativity inspire me every day, to the families who entrust me with their children's education, to the colleagues who challenge and support me, and to the mentors who have shaped my career: thank you. This book is dedicated to all of you, as a tribute to the transformative power of education and a call to action for us to create more equitable and empowering learning environments for all.

CONTENTS

I. INTRODUCTION

THE CHALLENGES FACED BY STRUGGLING URBAN SCHOOLS AND THE IMPORTANCE OF ADDRESSING THEM THROUGH A STUDENT-CENTERED APPROACH

In the United States, many urban schools are faced with significant challenges that can impact the academic success of their students. These challenges include over-crowded classrooms, limited resources, high teacher turnover, and a lack of family and community support. Additionally, students in urban schools often face societal and economic challenges such as poverty, homelessness, and exposure to violence, which can have a profound impact on their academic success.

Addressing these challenges is critical for ensuring that all students have access to a quality education that will prepare them for success in college, career, and life. However, traditional approaches to education have often fallen short in addressing the unique needs of urban students. To truly transform struggling urban schools, a student-centered approach is necessary.

A student-centered approach places the needs and interests of students at the center of all educational decision-making. This approach recognizes that students are more than just test scores and that they have unique backgrounds, experiences, and learning styles. By prioritizing the needs and interests of students, educators can create learning environments that are engaging, relevant, and effective.

One of the biggest challenges faced by struggling urban schools is a lack of resources. Often, these schools do not have the same funding and support as their suburban counterparts, which can result in overcrowded classrooms, outdated materials, and a lack of technology. However, a student-centered approach can help mitigate these challenges by prioritizing the needs of individual students and providing them with the resources they need to succeed.

In addition to a lack of resources, struggling urban schools often experience high teacher turnover rates. This can be due to a variety of factors, including low pay, high stress levels, and a lack of support. By prioritizing the needs and interests of students, a student-centered approach can help to alleviate some of the stress that teachers experience. For example, by providing opportunities for professional development and collaboration, educators can feel more supported and better equipped to meet the needs of their students.

Another challenge faced by struggling urban schools is a lack of family and community support. This can be due to a variety of factors, including language barriers, cultural differences, and a lack of trust. However, a student-centered approach can help to build bridges between schools and families by prioritizing communication and collaboration. By actively seeking out the perspectives and input of families and community members, educators can create a sense of partnership that can be instrumental in promoting student success.

Furthermore, students in urban schools often face societal and economic challenges that can have a significant impact on their academic success. For example, students who experience poverty, homelessness, or exposure to violence may struggle to focus on their studies or may lack the resources they need to succeed. However, a student-centered approach can help to address these challenges by providing students with the support they need to thrive. This can include access to counseling services, after-school programs, and other resources that can help students overcome the challenges they face.

To truly transform struggling urban schools, it is important to prioritize the needs and interests of students at all levels of the educational system. This includes creating policies and practices that promote student success, providing teachers with the support and resources they need to meet the needs of their students, and actively engaging families and community members in the educational process.

Ultimately, a student-centered approach is critical for ensuring that all students have access to a quality education that will prepare them for success in college, career, and life. By prioritizing the needs and interests of students, we can create learning environments that are engaging, relevant, and effective, and ensure that all students have the opportunity to reach their full potential.

II. UNDERSTANDING THE CONTEXT

THE CURRENT STATE OF URBAN EDUCATION AND ITS IMPACT ON STUDENT ACHIEVEMENT

The state of urban education in the United States has a significant impact on student achievement. Urban schools, which serve a large number of low-income and minority students, often face a variety of challenges that can impact the quality of education that students receive. These challenges can include high teacher turnover, limited resources, and a lack of family and community support. In this chapter, we will explore the current state of urban education and its impact on student achievement.

One of the biggest challenges facing urban schools is a lack of resources. Many urban schools do not have the same funding and support as their suburban counterparts, which can result in overcrowded classrooms, outdated materials, and a lack of technology. This lack of resources can have a significant impact on student achievement, as it can limit the opportunities that students have to learn and grow.

In addition to a lack of resources, urban schools often experience high teacher turnover rates. This can be due to a variety of factors, including low pay, high stress levels, and a lack of support. High teacher turnover rates can have a negative impact on student achievement, as it can result in a lack of consistency and stability in the classroom.

Furthermore, urban schools often face a lack of family and community support. This can be due to a variety of factors, including language barriers, cultural differences, and a lack of trust. A lack of family and community support can impact student achievement, as it can result in a lack of engagement and investment in the educational process.

Another challenge facing urban schools is the achievement gap. The achievement gap is the difference in academic performance between different groups of students, such as those from low-income families and those from more affluent families. The achievement gap is often wider in urban schools, as these schools serve a large number of low-income and minority students. This can have a significant impact on student achievement, as students from low-income families often have fewer resources and opportunities to learn.

Additionally, urban schools often face challenges related to school safety. Students in urban schools are often exposed to violence and other forms of trauma, which can impact their ability to learn and succeed in school. School safety is critical for promoting student achievement, as it provides a stable and secure learning environment where students can focus on their studies.

Despite these challenges, there are also many positive aspects of urban education that can impact student achievement. For example, urban schools often have more diverse student populations, which can provide students with a greater understanding and appreciation of different cultures and perspectives. Additionally, urban schools often provide students with opportunities to engage in real-world learning experiences, such as internships and community service projects, which can prepare them for success in college, career, and life.

To truly transform urban education and promote student achievement, it is important to address the challenges that urban schools face and build on their strengths. This includes providing urban schools with the resources and support they need to meet the needs of their students, creating policies and practices that promote equity and inclusion, and actively engaging families and community members in the educational process.

Ultimately, the state of urban education in the United States has a significant impact on student achievement. By recognizing and addressing the challenges facing urban schools, we can create learning environments that are engaging, relevant, and effective, and ensure that all students have the opportunity to reach their full potential.

THE ROLE OF SCHOOL LEADERSHIP IN CREATING A POSITIVE SCHOOL CULTURE AND FOSTERING STUDENT SUCCESS

School leadership plays a crucial role in creating a positive school culture and fostering student success. Effective leaders inspire and motivate their staff, students, and community to work together towards a common goal of academic success. In this chapter, we will explore the essential role of school leadership in creating a positive school culture and promoting student success.

First, school leaders are responsible for creating a positive school culture that is focused on student learning and success. This involves establishing a shared vision for the school, setting high expectations for students and staff, and creating a safe and supportive learning environment. The school culture should reflect the values and beliefs of the community and support the academic, social, and emotional growth of all students.

Effective school leaders also understand the importance of building relationships with students, staff, families, and community members. They establish an open-door policy, actively listen to feedback, and foster collaboration and communication. By building strong relationships, school leaders can gain support for their initiatives, increase student engagement, and improve academic performance.

In addition, school leaders must effectively manage resources, including personnel, budget, and time. They must make strategic decisions that allocate resources effectively and efficiently, and ensure that all stakeholders understand the rationale behind these decisions. By managing resources effectively, school leaders can ensure that students have access to the resources and support they need to be successful.

Another critical role of school leadership is to ensure that all students have access to high-quality instruction and support. Effective school leaders work to ensure that teachers have the resources, training, and support they need to deliver effective instruction to all students. They also provide targeted support to struggling students and create programs that promote academic success, such as tutoring, mentoring, and afterschool programs.

School leaders must also be advocates for their students and the school community. They must be knowledgeable about policy and legislative changes that impact education and work to ensure that their school is well represented and receives adequate funding and resources. By advocating for their school, school leaders can create a sense of pride and ownership within the community, and increase support for the school's initiatives and goals.

Furthermore, effective school leaders prioritize equity and inclusion, ensuring that all students have access to the resources, instruction, and support they need to be successful. They actively work to reduce achievement gaps and ensure that students from all backgrounds have the opportunity to excel. This involves creating policies and practices that promote equity and inclusion, such as targeted interventions for struggling students and the implementation of culturally responsive teaching practices.

Another critical role of school leadership is to promote a culture of continuous improvement. Effective school leaders encourage a growth mindset and promote a culture of ongoing learning and professional development for both teachers and administrators. They seek out best practices, innovative solutions, and new ideas to improve instruction and support student achievement. By promoting a culture of continuous improvement, school leaders can ensure that the school is constantly evolving to meet the needs of its students.

Finally, effective school leaders recognize the importance of data-driven decision-making. They regularly review student data to evaluate progress and identify areas of improvement. They use data to make informed decisions about instruction, support, and resource allocation, and they share data with teachers, staff, and families to promote transparency and accountability.

In conclusion, the role of school leadership

in creating a positive school culture and fostering student success is essential. Effective school leaders establish a shared vision, build strong relationships, manage resources effectively, promote high-quality instruction and support, advocate for their students and school community, prioritize equity and inclusion, promote a culture of continuous improvement, and use data-driven decision-making. By embodying these essential leadership qualities, school leaders can create schools that are engaging, relevant, and effective, and ensure that all students have the opportunity to reach their full potential.

4

THE IMPORTANCE OF RECOGNIZING AND ADDRESSING SYSTEMIC INEQUITIES

Systemic inequities are deeply embedded in our educational systems and have a significant impact on student achievement. These inequities are the result of a complex web of social, economic, and political factors that have historically disadvantaged students from certain racial, ethnic, and socioeconomic backgrounds. In this chapter, we will explore the importance of recognizing and addressing systemic inequities in order to create a more just and equitable education system.

First, it is essential to understand the ways in which systemic inequities manifest in our education system. These inequities include unequal access to resources, such as high-quality teachers, technology, and textbooks; disparate discipline practices that dispropor-tionately impact students of color and students with disabilities; and unequal opportunities for advanced coursework, extracurricular activ-ities, and enrichment programs. These inequities can have a significant impact on student achievement, creating disparities in academic outcomes and perpetuating cycles of poverty and inequality.

To address these inequities, it is essential to recognize and confront the underlying causes. This includes acknowledging the ways in which systemic racism, classism, and other forms of discrimination have contributed to these inequities, and actively working to dismantle these systems of oppression. It also involves acknowledging the lived experiences of students who have been impacted by these inequities and centering their voices and perspectives in the work of educational reform.

One key strategy for addressing systemic inequities is to create a more inclusive and culturally responsive curriculum. This involves incorporating diverse perspectives, experiences, and histories into the curriculum, and promoting critical thinking and dialogue about issues of power and privilege. It also involves creating opportunities for students to learn about and celebrate their own cultural identities and histories, and to develop a sense of pride and connection to their communities.

Another important strategy for addressing systemic inequities is to promote equity in resource allocation. This includes ensuring that all students have access to high-quality teachers, technology, textbooks, and other resources, regardless of their zip code or background. It also involves advocating for policies and funding that promote equity and inclusion, such as increased funding for low-income schools and targeted interventions for struggling students.

In addition, it is essential to address disparate discipline practices that disproportionately impact students of color and students with disabilities. This involves adopting restorative justice practices that focus on repairing harm and promoting positive behavior, rather than punitive measures that perpetuate cycles of exclusion and disengagement. It also involves providing targeted support and interventions for students who are struggling with behavioral or emotional issues, and creating a supportive and inclusive school culture that promotes positive relationships and student voice.

It is also important to address disparities in access to advanced coursework, extracurricular activities, and enrichment programs. This involves creating policies and practices that promote equity and inclusion, such as providing targeted support and interventions for students who are underrepresented in these programs, and creating opportunities for all students to participate in high-quality enrichment activities. It also involves promoting a culture of high expectations and excellence, and challenging traditional assumptions about which students are capable of success in advanced coursework and other challenging programs.

Finally, it is essential to involve students, families, and community members in the work of addressing systemic inequities. This involves creating opportunities for community engagement and dialogue, and building partnerships that promote collaboration and shared responsibility for student success. It also involves actively seeking out the perspectives and experiences of students and families who have been impacted by systemic inequities, and using this feedback to inform the work of educational reform.

In conclusion, recognizing and addressing systemic inequities is essential for creating a more just and equitable education system. This involves acknowledging the ways in which systemic racism, classism, and other forms of discrimination have contributed to these inequities, and actively working to dismantle these systems of oppression. However, this is only the first step.

III. CREATING INCLUSIVE
SCHOOL COMMUNITIES

5

BUILDING RELATIONSHIPS WITH STUDENTS AND FAMILIES

One of the most important aspects of creating a positive school culture and promoting student success is building strong relationships with students and families. When students feel connected to their teachers and administrators, they are more likely to feel engaged and motivated in their learning, and to develop a sense of belonging and connection to their school community. Similarly, when families feel involved and invested in their child's education, they are more likely to support their child's academic success and work collaboratively with school staff to promote positive outcomes.

In this chapter, we will explore strategies for building relationships with students and families, and the benefits of doing so.

First, it is essential to recognize the unique needs and experiences of individual students and families, and to approach relationships with empathy and understanding. This involves taking the time to listen to and acknowledge students' and families' perspectives and concerns, and working collaboratively to address any issues or challenges that may arise. It also involves recognizing and valuing the diversity of students' and families' experiences, and creating a culture of inclusion and respect.

One key strategy for building relationships with students is to prioritize relationship-building from the outset. This involves taking the time to get to know each student individually, and creating opportunities for students to share their interests, goals, and concerns with their teachers and peers. It also involves creating a culture of open communication, in which students feel comfortable approaching their teachers and administrators with any questions or concerns they may have.

Another important strategy for building relationships with students is to incorporate student voice into the school culture. This involves creating opportunities for students to have input into school policies and practices, and to take an active role in shaping their own learning experiences. It also involves promoting student leadership and agency, and encouraging students to take ownership of their own learning and growth.

Building relationships with families is also essential for promoting student success. This involves creating opportunities for families to be involved in their child's education, and to work collaboratively with school staff to support their child's learning and growth. It also involves recognizing and valuing the unique perspectives and experiences that families bring to the school community, and creating a culture of partnership and shared responsibility.

One key strategy for building relationships with families is to prioritize communication and outreach. This involves establishing regular communication channels, such as newsletters, parent-teacher conferences, and open houses, and providing information in multiple languages and formats to ensure that all families feel included and informed. It also involves creating opportunities for families to provide feedback and input into school policies and practices, and to be involved in decision-making processes.

Another important strategy for building relationships with families is to recognize and address the unique needs and challenges that families may face. This may include providing targeted support and interventions for families who are experiencing economic, health, or other challenges, and creating a culture of empathy and understanding. It also involves recognizing and valuing the cultural and linguistic diversity of families, and creating a welcoming and inclusive environment for all.

In addition to building relationships with individual students and families, it is also important to create a sense of community and connection within the school. This involves creating opportunities for students and families to come together and celebrate their shared experiences and achievements, and to feel connected to the broader school community. It also involves promoting a culture of respect and inclusivity, in which all members of the school community feel valued and supported.

In conclusion, building relationships with students and families is essential for creating a positive school culture and promoting student success. This involves prioritizing individualized support and attention, promoting student voice and agency, and creating a culture of partnership and shared responsibility. It also involves recognizing and valuing the unique needs and experiences of students and families, and promoting a culture of empathy and understanding. By prioritizing relationship-building, schools can create a sense of community and connection that supports student success and promotes positive outcomes for all members of the school community. When students feel connected to their teachers and peers, and when families feel invested and involved in their child's education, they are more likely to feel engaged, motivated, and supported in their learning. This, in turn, can lead to improved academic outcomes, higher graduation rates, and a greater sense of belonging and connection to the school community. By recognizing the importance of relationship-building and implementing strategies to support this, schools can create a positive, inclusive, and supportive environment that benefits all members of the school community.

6

CULTIVATING A POSITIVE SCHOOL CLIMATE AND CULTURE

A positive school climate and culture are essential for student success and the overall well-being of the school community. A positive school climate refers to the overall atmosphere and feel of the school, including how safe and welcoming it feels, while a positive school culture refers to the shared beliefs, values, and practices that guide behavior and decision-making in the school. Cultivating a positive school climate and culture requires intentional efforts by school leaders and staff, and can have a profound impact on student achievement, teacher retention, and overall school success.

To cultivate a positive school climate and culture, it is essential to establish clear and consistent expectations for behavior and interactions. This includes developing a school-wide code of conduct that is explicitly taught and reinforced through regular discussions and modeling by teachers and staff. It is also important to involve students in the development of this code of conduct, as this can help them feel more invested and accountable for upholding it.

Another critical aspect of building a positive school culture is creating opportunities for student leadership and voice. When students are given opportunities to lead and contribute to the school community, they are more likely to feel connected and invested in their learning. This can include providing opportunities for student-led clubs and organizations, student government, and other leadership roles. Additionally, creating space for student voice in decision-making processes, such as through regular town hall meetings or student surveys, can help ensure that student perspectives are heard and valued.

School leaders can also prioritize building positive relationships among staff members. This can include establishing regular opportunities for collaboration and professional development, as well as creating a culture of appreciation and recognition. When staff members feel supported and valued, they are more likely to be motivated and engaged in their work, which can have a positive impact on student achievement.

A positive school culture also involves celebrating diversity and promoting equity and inclusion. This means creating opportunities for students to learn about and celebrate their own cultures and identities, as well as those of others. Schools can also prioritize hiring a diverse staff and implementing culturally responsive teaching practices, which can help ensure that all students feel valued and represented in the school community.

Creating a positive school climate and culture also involves ensuring that all members of the school community feel physically and emotionally safe. This means taking steps to address bullying, harassment, and other forms of negative behavior. It also means providing access to resources and support for students who may be experiencing mental health or emotional issues. By creating a supportive and inclusive environment, schools can help ensure that all students feel valued and supported.

Finally, cultivating a positive school climate and culture involves regularly assessing and reflecting on school practices and policies. This means regularly collecting and analyzing data on student achievement and well-being, as well as soliciting feedback from students, families, and staff members. By regularly evaluating and improving upon school practices, leaders can help ensure that the school is continuously working towards its goal of providing a positive and supportive learning environment for all students.

In conclusion, building a positive school climate and culture is essential for creating an environment in which all students can thrive. By establishing clear expectations for behavior, providing opportunities for student leadership and voice, celebrating diversity and promoting equity and inclusion, creating a physically and emotionally safe environment, and regularly assessing and reflecting on school practices, leaders can create a positive, supportive, and inclusive learning environment for all members of the school community.

7

FOSTERING A SENSE OF COMMUNITY AND BELONGING

Fostering a sense of community and belonging is a critical component of creating a positive and inclusive school environment. A sense of community and belonging helps students feel connected to their school and motivated to learn. It can also help promote positive mental health outcomes and reduce negative behaviors like absenteeism and dropouts. In this chapter, we will explore strategies for fostering a sense of community and belonging in schools.

One of the most effective strategies for fostering a sense of community and belonging is through the development of a school-wide culture that values and prioritizes relationships. This can be accomplished by implementing school-wide initiatives such as restorative practices, where students are encouraged to take responsibility for their actions and make amends with those who have been affected by their behavior. By prioritizing relationships and promoting positive interactions, schools can create a more supportive and inclusive environment that values every member of the school community.

Another important strategy is to provide opportunities for students to get involved in extracurricular activities and clubs. Extracurricular activities provide students with a chance to explore their interests and passions, while also building relationships with peers who share those interests. Schools can also provide opportunities for student-led clubs and organizations, which can give students a sense of ownership and pride in their school.

Creating a positive and welcoming physical environment is also essential for fostering a sense of community and belonging. This means creating clean and well-maintained facilities, providing comfortable and functional classroom spaces, and promoting student artwork and accomplishments throughout the school. Schools can also consider creating common areas for students to gather and socialize, such as a student lounge or outdoor seating area.

Another important strategy for fostering a sense of community and belonging is through parent and family engagement. When parents and families are involved in their child's education, students are more likely to feel supported and motivated to succeed. Schools can provide opportunities for parents and families to get involved in school events, volunteer in the classroom, and provide feedback on school practices and policies. By involving families in the school community, schools can create a more supportive and collaborative environment that values the input and perspectives of all members.

Celebrating cultural and linguistic diversity is also important for fostering a sense of community and belonging. Schools can promote cultural awareness by providing opportunities for students to learn about and celebrate different cultures and traditions. This can include cultural assemblies, diversity celebrations, and multicultural curricular activities. By promoting cultural awareness and inclusivity, schools can help ensure that all students feel valued and represented in the school community.

Another effective strategy for fostering a sense of community and belonging is through the implementation of peer mentoring and support programs. Peer mentoring programs can provide students with additional support and guidance, as well as create opportunities for older students to serve as role models and leaders for younger students. Peer support groups, such as LGBTQ+ or racial affinity groups, can also provide students with a sense of connection and support.

It is also essential to prioritize the social-emotional learning (SEL) needs of students. SEL programs can provide students with the skills and tools needed to develop positive relationships, manage their emotions, and make responsible decisions. By prioritizing SEL, schools can help create a more supportive and empathetic environment that values the emotional well-being of all students.

Finally, it is important to regularly assess

and reflect on school practices and policies related to fostering a sense of community and belonging. This means collecting and analyzing data on student engagement, attendance, and achievement, as well as soliciting feedback from students, families, and staff members. By regularly evaluating and improving upon school practices, leaders can help ensure that the school is continuously working towards its goal of providing a supportive and inclusive learning environment for all students.

In conclusion, fostering a sense of community and belonging is critical for creating a positive and inclusive school environment. Strategies for fostering a sense of community and belonging include prioritizing relationships, providing opportunities for student involvement in extracurricular activities, creating a welcoming physical environment, engaging parents and families, celebrating cultural and linguistic diversity, implementing peer mentoring and support programs, prioritizing social-emotional learning, and regularly assessing and reflecting on school practices and policies. By implementing these strategies and prioritizing the well-being and engagement of every member of the school community, schools can help ensure that all students feel connected, supported, and motivated to succeed.

IV. AMPLIFYING STUDENT VOICE

8

STRATEGIES FOR EMPOWERING STUDENTS TO TAKE OWNERSHIP OF THEIR LEARNING

When students feel that they have a say in their education and that their voices are heard, they are more likely to be engaged and motivated in their learning. Empowering students to take ownership of their learning is a critical component of creating a student-centered and inclusive school community that is committed to closing the achievement gap. In this chapter, we will explore strategies for empowering students to take ownership of their learning.

1. Provide opportunities for student choice: Giving students choices in their learning can increase their

motivation and engagement.
Teachers can provide options for
assignments, projects, and
assessments that allow students to
showcase their strengths and
interests. For example, if students
are learning about ancient
civilizations, they could choose to
research and create a project on a
civilization that particularly
interests them.

2. Foster a growth mindset: Help
   students develop a growth mindset
   by encouraging them to see
   mistakes as opportunities to learn
   and grow. Teachers can provide
   feedback that focuses on effort and
   progress, rather than just grades or
   final products. When students feel
   that their effort is valued and that
   they can learn from their mistakes,
   they are more likely to take risks
   and try new things.

3. Create a culture of collaboration:
   Encouraging collaboration among
   students can help them develop

important skills such as communication, teamwork, and problem-solving. Teachers can facilitate group projects and discussions, provide opportunities for peer feedback, and promote a classroom culture that values diversity and inclusion.

4. Use inquiry-based learning: Inquiry-based learning is a student-centered approach that emphasizes questioning, exploration, and discovery. This approach can help students develop critical thinking and problem-solving skills, as well as a sense of ownership over their learning. Teachers can use inquiry-based learning by providing open-ended questions, encouraging investigation, and guiding students in their exploration.

5. Incorporate student-led conferences: Student-led conferences are a powerful way to empower students to take ownership of their learning. In

these conferences, students lead the discussion about their progress, goals, and achievements. Teachers can provide guidance and support, but the focus is on the student's voice and perspective. This approach helps students develop important skills such as self-reflection, self-evaluation, and self-advocacy.

6. Utilize technology: Technology can be a powerful tool for empowering students to take ownership of their learning. Teachers can use online platforms and tools that allow students to access information, collaborate with peers, and track their progress. For example, students can use online tools to create and share their work, participate in virtual discussions, and receive immediate feedback.

7. Promote student agency: Student agency refers to the degree of control and autonomy that students have over their learning. When

students feel that they have a say in their learning, they are more likely to be engaged and motivated. Teachers can promote student agency by providing opportunities for self-direction and choice, fostering student voice and choice, and encouraging student-led projects and initiatives.

8. Use formative assessment: Formative assessment is a process of gathering data on student learning that is used to inform and adjust instruction. Teachers can use formative assessment to help students understand their progress, identify areas for improvement, and set goals. This approach helps students develop metacognitive skills, such as self-reflection and self-regulation, and can increase their sense of ownership over their learning.

9. Promote reflection and self-evaluation: Reflection and self-evaluation are important skills for

empowering students to take ownership of their learning. Teachers can encourage students to reflect on their learning experiences, identify their strengths and weaknesses, and set goals for improvement. This approach helps students develop self-awareness, self-regulation, and a sense of responsibility for their learning.

10. Celebrate student achievements: Celebrating student achievements is an important way to recognize and reinforce positive behaviors and outcomes. When students feel valued and recognized for their accomplishments, they are more likely to take ownership of their learning and strive for continued success. In Chapter 8, we will discuss strategies for empowering students to take ownership of their learning and celebrate their achievements.

One important strategy is to involve

students in the goal-setting process. When students have a say in what they are working toward, they are more likely to be invested in the outcome. Teachers can work with students to set both academic and personal goals, and then provide opportunities for students to reflect on their progress and adjust their goals as needed.

Another way to empower students is to give them a voice in the classroom. This can be achieved through class discussions, group projects, and other collaborative activities that allow students to share their thoughts and ideas. Teachers can also incorporate student choice into assignments and assessments, allowing them to tailor their learning to their interests and strengths.

Providing regular feedback is another crucial aspect of empowering students. Feedback should be specific, timely, and focused on both strengths and areas for improvement. By providing feedback in this way, students can see the progress they are making and know what steps they need to take to continue improving.

Celebrating student achievements can take

many forms, from a simple verbal recognition to a more formal ceremony or event. Teachers can create a system for recognizing student accomplishments, such as a student of the week or month program, or by displaying student work in the classroom or school.

It is also important to recognize the achievements of the entire school community. Schools can create a culture of celebration by regularly acknowledging accomplishments, such as improved test scores, successful events, or community partnerships. By celebrating as a community, students can see the value in working together and feel a sense of pride in their school.

Finally, providing opportunities for student leadership can be a powerful way to empower students to take ownership of their learning. Student-led initiatives, such as a school garden, fundraising campaign, or service project, can provide students with leadership experience and a sense of ownership over their school community.

By implementing these strategies, teachers can create a learning environment in which students feel empowered to take ownership of

their learning and celebrate their achievements. This not only helps students succeed
academically, but also helps them develop the
confidence and self-efficacy needed for lifelong
success.

9

CREATING OPPORTUNITIES FOR STUDENTS TO VOICE THEIR OPINIONS AND IDEAS

L et us explore the importance of creating opportunities for students to voice their opinions and ideas, and how doing so can help to create a more inclusive and engaging learning environment.

Giving students a voice in their education is crucial to their success. When students feel that they have a say in their learning, they are more likely to be invested in the process and take ownership of their education. This can be achieved through a variety of methods, including class discussions, surveys, suggestion boxes, and student-led conferences.

One way to promote student voice is through class discussions. Teachers can create an open and welcoming environment where students feel comfortable sharing their thoughts and ideas. This can be achieved through the use of icebreakers and other activities designed to encourage collaboration and build trust. Teachers can also create guidelines for discussions that emphasize respect, active listening, and the importance of considering multiple perspectives.

Another way to promote student voice is through the use of surveys. Surveys can be used to gather information about student interests, learning preferences, and other important information that can inform instruction. Teachers can also use surveys to solicit feedback from students about their learning experience, such as what they found helpful, what they struggled with, and what they would like to see in the future.

Suggestion boxes are another way to promote student voice. By providing a space for students to share their ideas and concerns, teachers can create an open and transparent environment where students feel that their opinions are valued. Teachers can review the suggestions and respond to them, either individually or as a class, to show that they are taking the feedback seriously.

Student-led conferences are a powerful way to promote student voice and create a more student-centered learning environment. Instead of the traditional parent-teacher conference, students take the lead and share their progress, goals, and areas of strength and weakness. This approach allows students to take ownership of their learning and share their thoughts and ideas about their progress with their parents and teachers.

Another way to promote student voice is through the use of student councils or other student-led groups. These groups can provide a platform for students to voice their opinions and ideas about school policies, events, and other important issues. By empowering students to take a leadership role in the school community, teachers can help to create a more inclusive and engaging learning environment.

In addition to these strategies, teachers can also use technology to promote student voice. Online forums, discussion boards, and other digital platforms can provide a space for students to share their thoughts and ideas, even if they are not comfortable speaking up in class. Teachers can also use social media to connect with students and gather feedback about their learning experience.

Ultimately, creating opportunities for student voice requires a commitment to creating a student-centered learning environment. By valuing and prioritizing student input, teachers can create a more engaging and inclusive learning experience that empowers students to take ownership of their education. This not only helps students succeed academically, but also prepares them for success in the 21st century workforce, where collaboration, communication, and critical thinking skills are highly valued.

10

INCORPORATING STUDENT FEEDBACK INTO SCHOOL DECISION-MAKING

Here we will focus on the importance of incorporating student feedback into school decision-making processes. By actively soliciting and valuing student input, schools can create a more inclusive and student-centered environment that meets the needs of all students.

One way to incorporate student feedback into decision-making is through the use of surveys. Surveys can be used to gather information about student experiences, preferences, and opinions on a wide range of issues, from curriculum and instruction to school culture and climate. This information can then be used to inform school policies, practices, and initiatives.

Another way to incorporate student feedback is through the use of focus groups or student advisory committees. These groups can provide a platform for students to share their thoughts and ideas about school policies, events, and other important issues. By actively seeking out and valuing student input, schools can create a more collaborative and inclusive decision-making process.

Incorporating student feedback into decision-making can also help to address issues of equity and inclusion. By valuing the input of all students, including those who are historically marginalized or underrepresented, schools can create policies and practices that are more responsive to the needs of all students. This can include things like inclusive curriculum, targeted interventions for struggling students, and support for students who face barriers to academic success.

Another benefit of incorporating student feedback into decision-making is that it can help to build trust and communication between students and school leaders. When students feel that their voices are heard and valued, they are more likely to feel invested in their education and more willing to engage in the learning process.

To effectively incorporate student feedback into decision-making, it is important to create a culture of feedback and open communication. This can be achieved through the use of regular surveys, focus groups, and other opportunities for students to share their thoughts and ideas. Teachers and school leaders can also model the importance of feedback by soliciting feedback from colleagues and using that feedback to inform their own practice.

It is also important to ensure that feedback is used in a meaningful way. This means taking student input seriously and using it to inform decision-making processes. It also means providing regular feedback to students about how their input has been used and what changes have been made as a result of their feedback.

Incorporating student feedback can also be challenging, as it requires a commitment to active listening and an openness to changing established policies and practices. However, by valuing and prioritizing student input, schools can create a more inclusive and responsive learning environment that meets the needs of all students.

Finally, it is important to ensure that student feedback is solicited and incorporated in an ethical and responsible manner. This means protecting the privacy and anonymity of students who provide feedback and ensuring that the feedback is used in a way that benefits all students, rather than just a select few.

In conclusion, incorporating student feedback into school decision-making is an important way to create a more inclusive and student-centered learning environment. By actively seeking out and valuing student input, schools can create policies and practices that are more responsive to the needs of all students, and build trust and communication between students and school leaders. While incorporating student feedback can be challenging, it is an essential component of creating a culture of feedback and open communication, and ultimately, a more equitable and inclusive learning environment.

V. CLOSING THE ACHIEVEMENT GAP

11

EVIDENCE-BASED INSTRUCTIONAL STRATEGIES TO SUPPORT STUDENT SUCCESS

Teaching is the core of the educational process, and it is through high-quality instruction that students develop the knowledge and skills needed to succeed academically and beyond. In order to support student success, it is essential to use evidence-based instructional strategies that have been proven to be effective.

One evidence-based strategy that has been shown to improve student learning is the use of formative assessment. This involves assessing student understanding throughout a lesson, rather than just at the end. By doing so, teachers can adjust their instruction in real-time to better meet the needs of their students.

Another effective strategy is the use of differentiation. This involves tailoring instruction to meet the individual needs of each student. By providing differentiated instruction, teachers can help students who are struggling to catch up, while also challenging students who are excelling.

Collaborative learning is another strategy that has been shown to be effective. This involves having students work together in small groups or pairs to complete tasks and solve problems. Collaborative learning can improve student engagement and motivation, while also helping to build important social and interpersonal skills.

Project-based learning is another strategy that has gained popularity in recent years. This involves having students work on long-term, multidisciplinary projects that require them to apply their learning to real-world situations. Project-based learning can help students develop important critical thinking and problem-solving skills, while also encouraging creativity and collaboration.

Technology can also be used as an instructional tool to support student success. For example, educational software can provide immediate feedback to students and allow them to work at their own pace. Additionally, online resources and digital tools can help students stay engaged and motivated.

In addition to these evidence-based instructional strategies, it is important to ensure that instruction is culturally responsive. This involves taking into account the cultural backgrounds and experiences of students and incorporating them into instruction. By doing so, teachers can help students feel more connected to their learning and improve their engagement and motivation.

Another important aspect of effective instruction is the use of assessment to monitor student progress and identify areas of need. In addition to formative assessment, summative assessment can be used to measure student learning at the end of a unit or course. By using assessment data to guide instruction, teachers can better meet the needs of their students and ensure that they are making progress towards their goals.

Finally, it is important to ensure that instruction is delivered in an engaging and interactive manner. This can be achieved through a variety of instructional methods, such as the use of multimedia resources, hands-on activities, and student-centered learning approaches.

Incorporating these evidence-based instructional strategies into daily instruction can help support student success and promote achievement for all students. By tailoring instruction to meet the needs of individual students, providing opportunities for collaboration and project-based learning, and ensuring that instruction is culturally responsive and engaging, teachers can help their students achieve their full potential.

12

PROVIDING TARGETED SUPPORT FOR STRUGGLING STUDENTS

While creating an inclusive and supportive school community is essential to fostering student success, it is also important to recognize that some students may require additional support and intervention to achieve their potential. This chapter will explore evidence-based strategies and best practices for providing targeted support for struggling students.

Identifying struggling students is the first step in providing targeted support. Schools should establish a system for identifying struggling students, which may include regular assessments, observations, and communication with families. Once identified, struggling students should receive targeted support that is tailored to their individual needs.

One effective approach for supporting struggling students is to provide targeted interventions that focus on specific skill areas. For example, struggling readers may benefit from targeted interventions that focus on phonics, fluency, and comprehension. Similarly, struggling math students may benefit from targeted interventions that focus on foundational math skills, such as number sense and operations.

Another effective strategy for supporting struggling students is to provide small group or individualized instruction. This approach allows teachers to provide targeted support that is tailored to each student's individual needs. Teachers can also use this time to provide more intensive instruction and feedback, which can help struggling students make more significant gains in their learning.

Technology can also be a valuable tool for supporting struggling students. For example, educational software and online resources can provide students with additional opportunities to practice and reinforce key skills. Technology can also provide real-time feedback, which can be particularly helpful for students who struggle with self-monitoring and self-regulation.

In addition to providing targeted interventions, it is also important to create a positive and supportive learning environment for struggling students. This can include providing opportunities for students to connect with mentors, peers, and other supportive adults. It can also involve creating a safe and welcoming classroom environment where struggling students feel valued and supported.

Another key strategy for supporting struggling students is to provide opportunities for academic and social-emotional skill-building. For example, students who struggle with organization and time-management may benefit from targeted instruction and practice in these areas. Similarly, students who struggle with social skills may benefit from targeted instruction and practice in communication, collaboration, and conflict resolution.

Collaboration between teachers, families, and other support professionals is also essential for supporting struggling students. This can include regular communication and collaboration between teachers and families, as well as collaboration between teachers and other support professionals, such as school psychologists and social workers.

Finally, it is important to monitor the progress of struggling students regularly and adjust interventions as needed. This can include using data to track student progress and adjust interventions accordingly. It can also involve providing regular feedback to students and families about progress, as well as celebrating student achievements along the way.

In summary, providing targeted support for struggling students is essential for creating an inclusive and supportive learning environment that fosters student success. By identifying struggling students, providing targeted interventions and individualized instruction, creating a positive and supportive learning environment, providing opportunities for skill-building, and collaborating with families and other support professionals, schools can help struggling students achieve their potential and thrive in the classroom.

13

IMPLEMENTING DATA-DRIVEN INTERVENTIONS TO CLOSE THE ACHIEVEMENT GAP

One of the most significant challenges facing urban schools is the achievement gap between students of different racial, ethnic, and socioeconomic backgrounds. In this chapter, we will explore how data-driven interventions can help to close this gap and ensure that all students have access to a high-quality education.

The first step in implementing data-driven interventions is to collect and analyze data on student performance. This data can come from a variety of sources, including standardized tests, classroom assessments, and teacher observations. Once the data has been collected, it is essential to use it to identify areas where students are struggling and to develop targeted interventions to address those areas.

One effective intervention is the use of small-group instruction. Small groups allow teachers to provide individualized attention to students who are struggling in a particular area. This approach has been shown to be particularly effective for students who are struggling with reading and math. By grouping students based on their needs, teachers can provide targeted support that is tailored to their specific learning requirements.

Another intervention that has been shown to be effective is the use of technology-based programs that provide personalized instruction to students. These programs use algorithms to adapt to each student's learning level, providing targeted instruction that is tailored to their individual needs. One example of such a program is DreamBox, which uses games and other interactive activities to engage students and improve their math skills.

In addition to these targeted interventions, it is also important to provide a strong system of academic support to all students. This can include after-school tutoring programs, home-work help, and mentoring. These programs can be particularly effective for students who come from disadvantaged backgrounds and who may not have access to academic support at home.

It is also important to provide social and emotional support to students who are strug-gling academically. This can include counsel-ing, mentoring, and other programs that help students build resilience and develop coping skills. By addressing the social and emotional needs of students, we can create a supportive environment that helps all students succeed.

In order to be effective, data-driven inter-ventions must be supported by a strong culture of collaboration and teamwork. This requires the involvement of all stakeholders, including teachers, administrators, parents, and commu-nity members. By working together, these stakeholders can identify areas of need and develop interventions that are tailored to the specific needs of their students.

In addition to collaboration, it is also essen-tial to provide ongoing professional develop-ment to teachers and other school staff. This can include training on the use of data to inform instruction, as well as training on evidence-based instructional strategies. By providing ongoing support and training, we can ensure that teachers have the skills and knowledge they need to effectively implement data-driven interventions.

Finally, it is important to create a culture of high expectations for all students. This requires a belief that all students can succeed, regardless of their background or previous academic performance. By setting high expectations and providing the necessary support, we can create an environment in which all students can thrive.

In conclusion, data-driven interventions are a powerful tool for closing the achievement gap and ensuring that all students have access to a high-quality education. By collecting and analyzing data, developing targeted interventions, providing academic and social-emotional support, fostering collaboration and teamwork, providing ongoing professional development, and creating a culture of high expectations, we can create a school environment that supports the success of all students.

VI. SUSTAINING SUCCESS

14

STRATEGIES FOR MAINTAINING A CULTURE OF STUDENT VOICE AND EQUITY

C reating a culture of student voice and equity requires a sustained effort from school leaders, teachers, and staff. In this chapter, we will explore some strategies for maintaining this culture and ensuring that all students feel valued and supported.

1. Consistent implementation of evidence-based strategies: To maintain a culture of student voice and equity, it is essential to continue implementing the evidence-based strategies discussed in this book. By providing a consistent and reliable

approach to teaching and supporting students, schools can maintain an environment where students feel valued and supported.

2. Ongoing professional development: Education is an ever-evolving field, and it is essential for school staff to stay up-to-date on best practices and new research. Providing ongoing professional development opportunities for teachers and staff can help them stay informed and motivated to implement strategies that support student voice and equity.

3. Community partnerships: Engaging with community partners can help schools connect with families and students outside of the school day. By working with community organizations, schools can provide additional resources and support for students and families, which can help to maintain a culture of student voice and equity.

4. Data-driven decision-making: By regularly collecting and analyzing data, schools can make informed decisions about student support and ensure that all students are receiving the resources they need to succeed. This approach can help to maintain a culture of equity by ensuring that all students have access to the resources they need to succeed.

5. Regular student feedback: To maintain a culture of student voice, it is essential to regularly collect feedback from students about their experiences in school. This can be done through surveys, focus groups, or other methods. By regularly soliciting feedback, schools can ensure that students feel valued and heard.

6. Parent and family engagement: Engaging with parents and families is an essential component of maintaining a culture of student voice and equity. By working with

families, schools can provide additional support for students and ensure that families feel connected to the school community.

7. Student leadership opportunities: Providing opportunities for student leadership can help to maintain a culture of student voice and equity. By empowering students to take on leadership roles, schools can ensure that students are actively involved in the decision-making process and have a voice in the school community.

8. Inclusive curriculum: By providing an inclusive curriculum that reflects the diversity of the student body, schools can maintain a culture of equity and ensure that all students feel seen and heard. This can include incorporating diverse perspectives and voices into lessons and providing resources and materials that reflect the experiences of all students.

9. Restorative practices: Implementing restorative practices can help to maintain a culture of equity by ensuring that students are held accountable for their actions in a way that is fair and respectful. By providing opportunities for students to take responsibility for their actions and make amends, schools can help to maintain a positive and supportive culture.

10. Celebrating diversity and inclusion: Finally, it is essential to celebrate diversity and inclusion to maintain a culture of student voice and equity. By providing opportunities to celebrate the diverse backgrounds and experiences of students, schools can help to foster a sense of community and belonging that supports student success.

In conclusion, maintaining a culture of student voice and equity requires ongoing effort and attention from school leaders, teachers, and staff. By implementing evidence-based strategies, providing ongoing professional development, engaging with community partners, collecting and analyzing data, soliciting regular student feedback, engaging with families, providing opportunities for student leadership, creating an inclusive curriculum, implementing restorative practices, and celebrating diversity and inclusion, schools can create an environment where all students feel valued, supported, and able to succeed.

15

THE ROLE OF TEACHER AND STAFF PROFESSIONAL DEVELOPMENT IN SUSTAINING SUCCESS

Professional development is a critical component of sustained success in schools. It helps teachers and staff to stay current on best practices, improve their skills, and ultimately improve student achievement. In this chapter, we will explore the importance of teacher and staff professional development in sustaining a culture of student voice and equity.

Effective professional development should be ongoing, relevant, and targeted to specific needs. It should be differentiated based on the level of experience, knowledge, and skills of the teachers and staff. Professional development should also align with the school's goals and objectives and the specific needs of the students. Providing ongoing support and feedback is also crucial for sustained growth and development.

One strategy for effective professional development is to encourage collaboration and sharing of best practices among teachers and staff. Teachers and staff members who work together to solve problems, create lesson plans, and share resources are more likely to be successful in their teaching and support roles. This creates a culture of continuous learning and collaboration, which is essential to creating a sustainable and positive school environment.

Another strategy is to provide opportunities for teachers and staff to attend conferences, workshops, and training sessions. This not only helps them to stay current on the latest research and best practices but also provides a valuable opportunity to network and connect with colleagues in their field.

Teacher and staff professional development should also include training on cultural competence, equity, and inclusion. This includes understanding the needs of diverse student populations, recognizing and addressing systemic barriers, and developing strategies to ensure that all students feel safe and valued in the school community.

One effective approach to professional development is to use data to inform instruction and professional learning. By analyzing data on student performance, teachers and staff can identify areas where they need additional training or support. This allows professional development to be targeted and more effective in addressing the specific needs of the school and students.

In addition, it is important to provide ongoing coaching and support for teachers and staff. This can be done through observation and feedback, providing resources and tools for ongoing learning, and creating opportunities for peer-to-peer mentoring.

One challenge in sustaining professional development is finding the time and resources to make it happen. It is important for school leaders to prioritize and allocate resources to support ongoing professional development for their staff. This may include setting aside dedicated time for professional development, providing funding for conference attendance and other training opportunities, and providing incentives for staff who demonstrate a commitment to ongoing learning and development.

Finally, school leaders should model a commitment to ongoing learning and professional development. By engaging in professional development opportunities and demonstrating a commitment to continuous learning, school leaders can create a culture where ongoing learning and growth are valued and celebrated.

In conclusion, teacher and staff professional development is critical to sustaining a culture of student voice and equity. Effective professional development should be ongoing, relevant, and differentiated, and should include opportunities for collaboration, data analysis, and cultural competence training. School leaders should prioritize and allocate resources for professional development and model a commitment to ongoing learning and growth. By investing in professional development, schools can improve student achievement and create a positive and sustainable school culture.

16

ENSURING ONGOING COMMUNICATION AND COLLABORATION WITH FAMILIES AND THE COMMUNITY

In a successful school community, communication and collaboration are key. In Chapter 5, we discussed the importance of building relationships with families and the community, but it is equally important to maintain ongoing communication and collaboration throughout the school year. In this chapter, we will explore strategies for ensuring that families and the community are kept informed and involved in the school's work and progress.

One of the most important ways to ensure ongoing communication and collaboration is to establish multiple channels for communication. This might include regular newsletters or email updates, a school website or blog, social media accounts, or even a school app. These channels can be used to share information about upcoming events, academic progress, and other important updates. Additionally, having a clear and accessible process for families to reach out with questions or concerns is critical.

Another important aspect of ongoing communication and collaboration is involving families and the community in school decision-making. This might include inviting family and community members to participate in school committees, advisory boards, or other decision-making groups. This can help ensure that a diversity of voices and perspectives are represented and can lead to more equitable and effective decision-making.

Community partnerships are another key aspect of ensuring ongoing communication and collaboration. By working with local organizations, businesses, and community members, schools can provide opportunities for students that might not otherwise be available. This might include internships, mentorships, or other career exploration opportunities. Additionally, partnering with local organizations can help bring additional resources and expertise into the school community.

One effective way to involve families and the community in school work is through family engagement events. These might include open houses, family nights, or other events designed to give families an opportunity to connect with teachers and staff and learn more about the school's work. These events can also be used to gather feedback and ideas from families about ways to improve the school and ensure that it is meeting the needs of all students.

In addition to involving families and the community in decision-making and events, it is also important to solicit feedback and input from them. This might include surveys, focus groups, or other forms of feedback. By actively seeking out feedback and input, schools can ensure that they are meeting the needs of all students and families.

Finally, it is important to celebrate and highlight the accomplishments of the school community. This might include showcasing

student work or accomplishments, high-
lighting the work of teachers and staff, or
sharing stories of success and progress. By celebrating the successes of the school community,
families and community members are more
likely to feel invested in the school's work and
motivated to continue to support it.

In conclusion, ensuring ongoing communication and collaboration with families and the
community is critical to creating a successful
school community. By establishing multiple
channels for communication, involving families and the community in decision-making
and events, soliciting feedback and input, and
celebrating successes, schools can create a
culture of collaboration and support that is
focused on meeting the needs of all students.

VII. CONCLUSION

17

BUILDING INCLUSIVE SCHOOL COMMUNITIES FOR TRANSFORMING URBAN SCHOOLS

In this final chapter, we bring together the key themes and strategies discussed throughout the book and emphasize the importance of creating inclusive school communities that value student voice and prioritize equity in order to transform struggling urban schools into successful and thriving learning environments. We have explored the challenges faced by urban schools and the role of leadership in creating a positive school culture and fostering student success. We have discussed the importance of recognizing and addressing systemic inequities, building relationships with students and families, and cultivating a sense of community and belonging. We have also looked at strategies for empowering students to take ownership of their learning, incorporating student feedback into school decision-making, and providing targeted support for struggling students.

One of the key takeaways from this book is that students must be at the center of all efforts to transform struggling urban schools. This means prioritizing relationship-building, creating a positive school climate and culture, and fostering a sense of community and belonging. When students feel valued, supported, and heard, they are more likely to be engaged in their learning and motivated to succeed.

Another critical factor in creating successful and thriving urban schools is addressing systemic inequities. This requires a deep understanding of the root causes of educational disparities and a commitment to equity in all aspects of school life. It also requires ongoing reflection and self-examination to ensure that we are not perpetuating inequities through our own biases and assumptions.

Empowering students to take ownership of

their learning is another essential component of creating successful and thriving urban schools. This means providing opportunities for students to voice their opinions and ideas, and incorporating their feedback into school decision-making. It also means implementing evidence-based instructional strategies to support student success and providing targeted support for struggling students.

Effective teacher and staff professional development is also critical to sustaining success in urban schools. This means providing ongoing opportunities for professional learning and growth, and supporting teachers and staff in implementing evidence-based instructional strategies and interventions.

Finally, ongoing communication and collaboration with families and the community are essential for building inclusive school communities. This means recognizing the important role that families and community members play in supporting student success, and actively seeking their input and involvement in school decision-making.

In conclusion, creating successful and

thriving urban schools requires a holistic approach that prioritizes student voice, equity, and inclusive school communities. By working together, we can transform struggling urban schools into places where all students can succeed and thrive.

ABOUT THE AUTHOR

Uche L. Njoku is an experienced educator and financial literacy advocate based in New York City. With over two decades of experience in education, including as a former principal in the New York City public school system, he has a deep understanding of the challenges facing young people in today's economy. In addition to his work as an educator, Njoku is a frequent speaker and commentator on financial literacy and crypto education, and has been featured in a variety of media outlets. He is a passionate advocate for empowering young people with the knowledge and skills they need to succeed in today's rapidly evolving world.

Made in the USA
Middletown, DE
28 February 2023

25579560R00060